Contents

Some words are shown in bold, **like this**.
You can find out what they mean by looking
in the glossary.

What is democracy?

Outside a village hall, people are queuing up. They are waiting for their turn to **vote** in a national **election**. Elections are a part of life in a democratic country such as the United Kingdom. Voting is an important way for people to have their say in how the country is run.

The birth of democracy

Democracy began over 2,000 years ago in ancient Greece. "Democracy" comes from Greek words meaning "people" and "power". Instead of being ruled by kings, the city of Athens was governed by its people. All male **citizens** were allowed to join an assembly. The assembly met regularly to vote on important issues and make laws.

This woman is posting a vote in a **ballot** box. This is one way to vote.

DEMOCRACY
IN THE UK

Nancy Dickmann

raintree
a Capstone company — publishers for children

Raintree is an imprint of Capstone Global Library Limited, a company incorporated in England and Wales having its registered office at 264 Banbury Road, Oxford, OX2 7DY – Registered company number: 6695582

www.raintree.co.uk
myorders@raintree.co.uk

Edited by Clare Lewis
Designed by Cynthia Della-Rovere
Picture research by Eric Gohl
Production by Laura Manthe
Originated by Capstone Global Library

Printed and bound in India

ISBN 978 1 4747 6221 2 (hardback)

ISBN 978 1 4747 6223 6 (paperback)

British Library Cataloguing in Publication Data
A full catalogue record for this book is available from the British Library.

Acknowledgements
We would like to thank the following for permission to reproduce photographs:Alamy: Gordon Shoosmith, 4, Jeff Morgan, 10, Tim Scrivener, 11, Tony Watson, 8; AP Photo: Sang Tan, cover (bottom right); Getty Images: Sam Mellish, 26, Stringer/Anthony Devlin, 22; Newscom: picture-alliance/dpa/Michael Kappeler, 23, Reuters/Peter Nicholls, 9, Reuters/Pool, 14, Reuters/Tim Wimborne, 19, ZUMA Press/Dan Kitwood, 13, ZUMA Press/Howard Jones, 17, ZUMA Press/I-Images, 27, ZUMA Press/Lewis Whyld, 15, ZUMA Press/Pa, cover (top left), ZUMA Press/Stefan Rousseau, 21, ZUMA Press/Stephen Lock, 28; Shutterstock: 1000 Words, cover (top right), Anthony Shaw Photography, cover (bottom left), Complexli, 24, Daniel Heighton, 20, DGLimages, 6, Dmitry Kalinovsky, 7, Drop of Light, 18, jax10289, 16, lonndubh, 25, Mark Scott, cover (middle), back cover (top), 1, Monkey Business Images, back cover (bottom left), 5, Ulmus Media, back cover (bottom right), Zoltan Gabor, 12

Design Elements: Shutterstock.

We would like to thank Simon Bulmer from the Department of Politics at the University of Sheffield for his invaluable help in the preparation of this book.

Every effort has been made to contact copyright holders of material reproduced in this book. Any omissions will be rectified in subsequent printings if notice is given to the publisher.

Modern democracy

We use a similar system today, but the UK is too big a country to copy it exactly. It wouldn't be practical for the entire country to vote on every single issue. Instead, we have what is called a **representative democracy**. Citizens vote for people who will represent them – and their views – in **government**. The modern system allows people's voices to be heard. Democracy is one of our core British values.

Democracy in action

As part of our democracy, every few years the people vote for Members of **Parliament** (**MPs**) who represent their views. The nation also sometimes votes directly on important issues. But democracy is also in action all around you. Voting for representatives on a school **council** is a form of democracy. So is taking a vote among your friends to decide which film to watch!

Do you ever take a vote in your classroom? That is a form of democracy!

Local government

The central government deals with big issues such as defence and **foreign relations**. But many of the issues that affect our everyday lives are controlled by local government.

Why go local?

Different parts of the country have different needs. Many decisions affect just a small number of people. It wouldn't be efficient for the central government to look after everything. There are many areas where it works better to have local people make decisions. They know their community and its needs better than anyone.

Some funding for schools is controlled by local government.

What local governments do

The list of services provided by local governments is very long! In different parts of the UK, local governments have slightly different responsibilities. These are some of the most common areas that local governments oversee:

- **planning** decisions about new buildings and businesses
- transport (from bus shelters to building new roads)
- fire and public safety
- libraries, leisure centres and museums
- council housing
- services for children, including some aspects of education
- social care for elderly or disabled **residents**
- keeping streets clean
- planning for natural disasters such as floods

Local governments are responsible for making sure waste is collected. They also encourage recycling.

☑ Your opinion counts!

Local governments are responsible for a lot. When they choose how to spend their budget, they must decide what is most important for the community. What do you think are the most important services? How would you choose how to spend the budget?

Local governments receive money from the central government. They also collect money from residents and local businesses in the form of tax. They use this to pay for the services they provide.

Community and town councils

The lowest level of local government is made up of community or town councils. In some places they are called parish councils. Their members are usually elected by the local community. It is a part-time job, and many of the councillors are not paid. They are responsible for things such as allotments, play areas and littering.

Parish councils often use noticeboards to notify residents about issues.

Larger councils

In some parts of the UK, there are two higher levels of local government. The lower of these two levels is sometimes called a district council. In other areas there are city or borough councils instead. Above them is the county council, which covers a larger area. In other places, there is only a single council, which looks after all of the local services. This is called a unitary authority.

Local people elect the members of these councils. The councillors usually stay in their roles for four years. Most of them will belong to a national **political party**. However, some people are elected to local councils as independent **candidates**. They are not linked to a political party.

Mayors and council leaders

Many councils are headed up by a council leader, who is elected by the other councillors. The council leader takes the lead in making decisions. In other places, such as London and Greater Manchester, the residents vote for a **mayor** instead. Many cities also have a lord mayor, who represents the council at ceremonial events. The lord mayor is usually chosen by the councillors. He or she has no political power.

A lord mayor often wears a heavy chain at official events.

Making decisions

Councils make decisions in different ways. In some councils, the council leader **appoints** other councillors to form a **cabinet**. Each cabinet member looks after a different area, such as housing or education. The leader and cabinet make decisions together. In other councils, groups of councillors form committees. Each committee focuses on a particular topic. The committees make some decisions themselves. If they can't agree on an issue, the full council may vote on it.

Councils often try to find out residents' opinions before making decisions. This might mean putting on a public display of plans for a new shopping centre or housing development. The public can have their say before a decision is made. This process is called consultation.

Residents might attend council meetings. They want to hear the **debate** and have their say.

Helping immigrants

In recent years, the town of Boston in Lincolnshire has had a huge rise in **immigration**. Thousands of people from eastern European countries such as Poland, Lithuania and Latvia have arrived. Many of them do vital work on farms, where vegetables are grown.

The arrival of so many immigrants has created new needs, and the Boston Borough Council is working to provide for them.

For example, they are working with local schools to make sure there are enough English language courses for the people who need them. They are making sure that official documents are translated into other languages. Officials are working together with the Eastern European immigrants and the local population to break down barriers. They want to make sure that everyone can live together peacefully.

Lincolnshire's farms depend on immigrant workers, especially at harvest time.

National government

Each local government only covers a fairly small area. Big decisions that affect the whole country, such as immigration, are made by the national government.

The House of Commons and House of Lords both meet in London, at the Houses of Parliament.

Parliament

The UK has a Parliament for making laws and checking the work of the government. Parliament is divided into the House of Commons and the House of Lords. The House of Commons is made up of 650 Members of Parliament, called MPs for short. Each one represents an area called a **constituency** and is elected by the public.

Working together

Members of the House of Lords are not elected. Most of them are appointed. A small number are members of the **aristocracy**, and some are bishops. Some former MPs are appointed to the House of Lords after serving in the House of Commons.

The two houses work together to make and pass laws. Proposed laws are called bills. All bills must be agreed on by both houses before they can become law. Members will debate a bill and suggest changes before voting on it.

The monarch

The UK is a constitutional monarchy, which means that we have a king or queen as well as a democratic government. The monarch opens and dissolves (closes) Parliament and gives official approval to Parliament's decisions.

Becoming an MP

In order to stand for election as an MP, you must be 18 years old or over. You must be a British or Irish citizen, or a citizen of a **Commonwealth** country with permission to stay in the UK. Some groups, such as members of the police or the armed forces, are not allowed to stand.

The House of Lords has about 800 members.

13

What is the government?

MPs usually belong to a political party – a group of people with similar ideas about how the country should be run. The two largest parties are Labour and the Conservatives. The leader of the party that has the most MPs in the House of Commons becomes the **prime minister**.

The prime minister chooses a small group called the cabinet, made up of MPs and members of the House of Lords. Together, they make up the government. Each member has a different area to oversee, which is called a portfolio. They include health, transport and foreign relations. The prime minister and the cabinet make decisions about how the country will be run. However, they cannot pass new laws or taxes without Parliament's agreement.

The cabinet usually meets once a week. The prime minister, Theresa May, leads the meeting.

From 2010 to 2015, the UK government was a coalition between the Conservatives (led by David Cameron, left) and the Liberal Democrats (led by Nick Clegg, right).

Coalition governments

If one party doesn't win enough seats to have a **majority**, they might form a **coalition** with another party. In a coalition government, two or more parties will agree to work together. MPs from both parties can serve in the cabinet.

The civil service

Running the country is a big job. The government cannot do everything by itself. An organization called the civil service helps carry out the government's decisions. Part of the civil service advises ministers on policy. The civil service is in charge of services such as paying benefits and pensions and issuing driving licences. Civil servants are not elected. Many of them work in the same department for years, becoming experts in their field.

Devolution

The United Kingdom is made up of four nations and regions: England, Scotland, Wales and Northern Ireland. For many years, the decisions made in London affected the entire country. But in the 1990s, the residents of Scotland, Wales and Northern Ireland voted to have their own **assemblies**.

The National Assembly for Wales meets in the Senedd building in Cardiff.

These assemblies have the power to make their own decisions on issues such as education, transport and farming. This is called devolution. The devolved assemblies are made up of representatives who are elected by the public. By putting power in the hands of national assemblies, local needs can be taken into account when making decisions.

Some powers are still reserved for the central government in London. These include immigration, citizenship and defence. The decisions made by Parliament in these areas affect all four nations and regions.

Tuition fees

Starting in 1962, a university education was free for full-time students across the entire UK. Then, in 1998, the government passed a law that introduced tuition fees. This law applied in all the home nations. However, the Scottish Parliament was formed the very next year. It had the power to make decisions about education in Scotland.

The Scottish Parliament eventually agreed that the Scottish government should pay for university education for Scottish students. (Technically, tuition fees are still charged, but a government agency pays them.) It is only free for Scottish students studying at Scottish universities. This is an example of how devolution can lead to different policies in different parts of the UK.

Many young people want tuition fees to be scrapped in all parts of the UK.

Working with other countries

Our government makes agreements with other countries. It also looks after the interests of British citizens who live abroad.

International cooperation

Countries around the world work together to solve problems peacefully. Nearly all the world's countries, including the UK, are members of the United Nations. The UK is also a member of the Commonwealth, a smaller group of nations that includes Canada and Australia. It is part of NATO, an organisation of countries including the USA that have agreed to help defend each other. The UK government sends representatives to all of these organisations. They make sure that Britain has a say in making decisions.

Representatives from countries around the world meet at the United Nations headquarters in New York City.

In Commonwealth countries, embassies are called high commissions.

Embassies

The UK government has staff working in many other countries. Their headquarters in a foreign country is called an embassy. The staff at an embassy discuss issues with local officials. They also help British citizens who are living or travelling in those countries.

Foreign relations

Our relationships with other countries are managed by a department called the Foreign Office. It is led by the Foreign Secretary, who is appointed by the prime minister. Staff from the Foreign Office meet with representatives of other countries. They agree deals that help keep the UK safe, such as sharing information about terrorism. They also sign agreements that help British business.

 **Your opinion counts!**

The foreign secretary, ambassadors and representatives to the UN are not directly elected to their roles. Instead, they are appointed. Do you think that the public should have a voice in choosing people for these important roles?

Elections and referendums

Democracy is all about giving the people a voice in making decisions. The best way to do this is to vote!

General elections

At an election, voters are given a ballot that lists the candidates. They mark it to show which candidate they choose. The most important elections in the UK are general elections, when MPs are chosen. Depending on the result, a new government is formed after the election.

General elections usually take place every 5 years. In a general election, people vote for a candidate in their local constituency. They do not vote directly for the prime minister.

Polling places are often set up in schools, village halls or other public buildings.

London was the first city in the UK to have a directly elected mayor in 2000. More recently, Sadiq Khan was elected to the post in 2016, replacing Boris Johnson.

Other elections

Local councillors serve for four years, but local elections do not happen at the same time in all areas. Elections for the Scottish Parliament and the Northern Ireland Assembly take place every four years. For the National Assembly of Wales, it is every five years. There are also elections for mayor in some areas.

Who can vote?

To vote in a general election, you must be 18 or older. You must also be a British citizen, or an Irish or Commonwealth citizen living in the UK. Citizens from European Union (EU) countries who are living in the UK can't vote in general elections, but they can vote in local elections. They can also vote in elections for the regional assemblies in Scotland, Wales and Northern Ireland.

Voting systems

There are different ways of deciding the winner of an election. The most common voting system in the UK is called First Past the Post (FPTP). MPs and local councillors in England and Wales are elected this way. Voters are given a list of candidates on the ballot. They choose one, and the candidate with the most votes wins. If there are several candidates, it is possible to receive fewer than half of the votes and still win.

The candidates gather while the returning officer announces the result.

Proportional representation

The other main type of voting is called Proportional Representation (PR). It is used to elect representatives to regional assemblies, and local councillors in Scotland and Northern Ireland. In some systems of PR, voters rank the candidates in order of preference. In others, they vote for a party.

In Germany, the parliament is elected using a mixture of FPTP and PR.

A fair result?

FPTP is simple, but it makes it difficult for small parties to win seats. Although they may win many votes across the country, they don't get enough in any one constituency. In the 2015 general election, 36.9% of all votes cast were for Conservative party candidates. They won 331 seats, which is 51% of the available seats. The UK Independence Party (UKIP) won 12.6% of votes nationwide, but they didn't win a single seat. Some people are campaigning to change the voting system because they think it is unfair.

 Your opinion counts!

Do you think that FPTP is a good system? Or do you think it would be better to use a system where the seats are shared out in the same percentages as the overall vote?

In the Scottish independence referendum, 55% of voters chose to remain in the UK.

Referendums

A **referendum** is a different kind of vote. Instead of choosing a candidate, voters express their opinion on a particular issue. Often the ballot paper will ask a simple question, such as "Should Scotland be an independent country?" The voter then marks either the box for "yes" or the box for "no".

Referendums are simple, but they are rare. The government makes most decisions itself. It wouldn't be practical for the whole country to vote on minor issues. Referendums are reserved for important decisions, such as independence, leaving the EU, setting up regional assemblies, or changing the voting system. There have only ever been three referendums that affected the entire UK. There have also been referendums that affected only one of the home nations, such as the Scottish independence referendum in 2014.

Leaving the EU

▶ The EU is a group of countries working together to promote peace and improve trade. In 1975, in the first ever UK-wide referendum, 66% of people voted to remain in the European Economic Community (the former name of the EU). In 2016, another referendum was held to decide whether to leave or remain in the EU. The "leave" vote won, by 51.9% to 48.1%.

The vote showed splits in opinion across the country. In Scotland and Northern Ireland, voters backed "remain", but "leave" won in England and Wales. Age made a difference to the way people voted, too. About 73% of voters aged 18–24 voted to remain, while 60% of voters aged over 65 voted to leave.

People took to the streets to show their view on remaining or leaving.

Getting involved

Elections are important, but they are not the only way to have your say. Even if you are not old enough to vote, you can still get involved in local issues.

Think local!

For many people, the issues that they feel most strongly about, such as transport or rubbish collections, are local. Local residents often work together to persuade their council to make changes. They may form groups that focus on a particular issue, such as safety for cyclists or protecting a local green space.

Making banners or holding a rally can raise awareness about an issue.

Stay informed

Many local council meetings are open to the public. There is often time set aside for councillors to answer questions from the public. Even if you can't attend a meeting, you can still stay informed. Before a meeting, councils usually publish the list of topics to be discussed on their website. Afterwards, they publish a record of their discussions.

Contact your MP

An MP debates national issues in Parliament, but that is only part of their job. They also have a responsibility to support their constituents. They can offer help and advice on individual problems, such as with benefits or immigration. They can also get involved in local issues. You can contact your MP by post or email.

MPs spend time in their constituencies, where they can meet one-on-one with the people they represent.

Questions in Parliament

MPs can ask questions in the House of Commons. They can raise issues that affect their constituents with cabinet ministers. Every Wednesday, at a session called Prime Minister's Questions, MPs can pose their questions directly to the prime minister.

Petitions

A **petition** is a request for action on a particular issue. Parliament has an online petition system. Anyone can set up a petition, as long as they are a British citizen or UK resident. Then people can sign it online. If a petition gets 10,000 signatures, the government will respond. If it gets 100,000 signatures, it may be debated in Parliament.

Democracy and you

Democracy gives you a say in how the country is run. If you think something is wrong, don't just grumble – do something about it! You may be able to make a real difference.

People sign a petition to show their support for it.

Government in the UK

This chart shows the general structure of government in the UK. Depending on where you live, the set-up might be slightly different. For example, if you live in England, there is no devolved assembly (see page 16). And if you live in an area that has a unitary authority (see page 8), there won't be separate district and county councils.

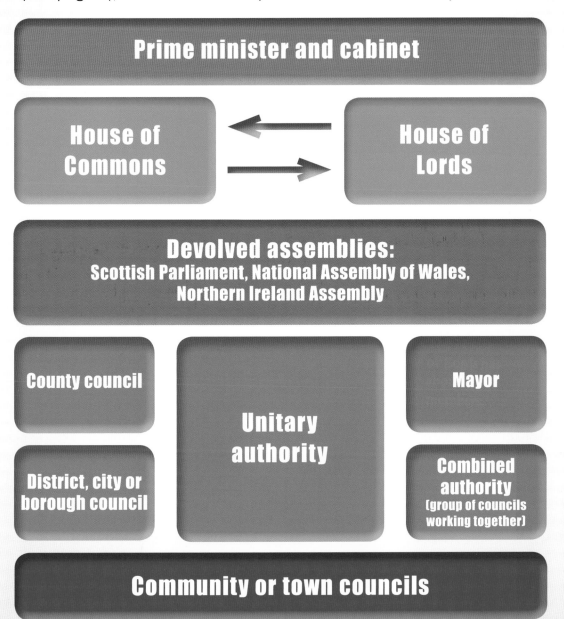

Prime minister and cabinet

House of Commons

House of Lords

Devolved assemblies:
Scottish Parliament, National Assembly of Wales, Northern Ireland Assembly

County council

Mayor

Unitary authority

District, city or borough council

Combined authority
(group of councils working together)

Community or town councils

Glossary

appoint give someone a particular role or job

aristocracy class of people with a high social position who pass their titles to their children

assembly body that meets to debate issues and decide on new laws

ballot piece of paper on which people who are voting enter their choices

cabinet group of officials who give advice to the head of a government

candidate person who puts himself or herself forward to be elected to office

citizen person who is a member of a country and has full rights, either because of being born there or having been declared a member by law

coalition government in which two or more parties agree to work together

Commonwealth group of countries, including the UK, which work together to promote democracy, trade, peace and human rights

constituency district that is represented by an elected official such as an MP

council group of elected officials who make decisions about public matters, often at a local level

debate discuss the different sides of a subject or issue

election process of choosing a person for office by voting

foreign relations way in which our country deals with other countries

government group of people that has the power to make important decisions that affect all people living in a community or country

immigration act of coming to live permanently in a foreign country

majority more than half of the votes or seats available

mayor head of a council or group of councils, who is directly elected by the people

MP (short for Member of Parliament) elected member of the House of Commons

Parliament highest law-making body in the UK, which consists of the House of Commons and the House of Lords

petition formal written request for action that is signed by many people

planning control of town or city development by a government authority, which grants licences for building or changing property

political party group of people with similar views who put forward candidates in elections and aim to form or take part in a government

prime minister head of the government, who leads the cabinet

referendum a vote on a question or issue, rather than for a candidate

representative democracy system of government in which the public elect people to represent their views in government

resident person who lives in a particular area

vote choose a candidate or register an opinion on a question

Find out more

Books

All About Politics (Big Questions), Andrew Marr (Dorling Kindersley, 2016)

Brexit: Britain's Decision to Leave the European Union, Daniel Nunn (Raintree, 2016)

Democracy (Exploring British Values), Catherine Chambers (Raintree, 2017)

Government and Democracy (Our Values), Charlie Ogden (Book Life, 2016)

Let's Vote on It! (British Values), Christopher Yeates (Gresham Books, 2016)

Vote for Me!: How Governments and Elections Work Around the World, Louise Spilsbury (Wayland, 2017)

What Does it Mean to Be British?, Nick Hunter (Raintree, 2016)

Websites

Go here to see how online petitions work, or even write your own:
www.gov.uk/petition-government

This website will help you find your MP and tell you how to contact him or her:
www.parliament.uk/mps-lords-and-offices/mps/

Find your local councillors here:
www.gov.uk/find-your-local-councillors

Find some fascinating questions and answers about voting and elections in the UK:
www.parliament.uk/about/faqs/house-of-commons-faqs/elections-faq-page/

Want to know more about how government works? Try this website:
www.gov.uk/government/how-government-works

Places to visit

Houses of Parliament
Westminster
London SW1A 0AA

Senedd (National Assembly of Wales)
Cardiff
CF10 4PZ

Scottish Parliament Building
Edinburgh
EH99 1SP

Parliament Buildings (Northern Ireland Assembly)
Belfast
BT4 3ST

Index